I CAN MAKE

DOLLS' CLOTHES

Easy-to-follow patterns to make clothes and accessories for your favorite doll

I CAN MAKE

DOLLS' CLOTHES

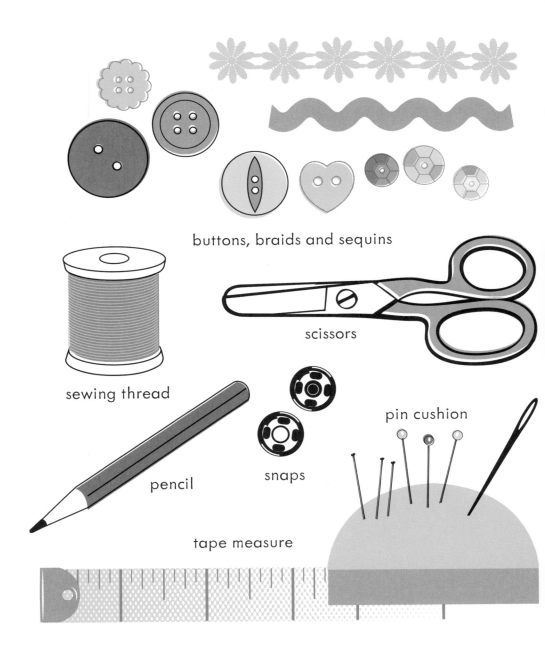

buttons, braids and sequins

scissors

sewing thread

pencil

snaps

pin cushion

tape measure

essentials kit

let's sew

All the designs in this book fit a regular 30 cm (12 in) fashion doll. They will also fit a slightly bigger or smaller doll.

Follow the simple step-by-step instructions to make stylish new outfits for your favorite doll. The sewing tips starting on page 168 will help you on your way.

Why not start collecting fabric scraps, braids and buttons to customize your doll's outfits? Keep them safe in your sewing box, along with your sewing kit.

There are design ideas to inspire you on page 164. You'll soon be creating your own designs!

remember
Always point needles and pins away from you. If you can't cut your fabric with rounded scissors, ask a grown-up to help you use some sharper ones.

a tunic top

12 x 18 cm (5 x 7 in) of fabric

a 12 x 9 cm (5 x 3½ in) piece of tracing paper

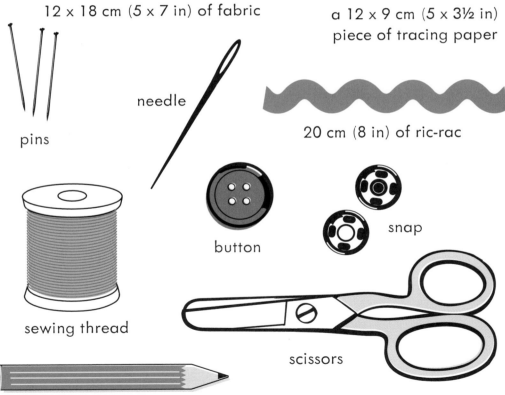

pins

needle

20 cm (8 in) of ric-rac

sewing thread

button

snap

scissors

pencil

you will need

a piece of fabric

some tracing paper

some pins

a needle

some ric-rac

sewing thread

a button

a snap

a pencil

and a pair of scissors

First you need to make a pattern.

Fold the tracing paper in half.

Place the folded edge against
the dotted line on the page.

Carefully trace the outline on
the page onto the tracing paper.

Cut around the solid line on the
tracing paper. Don't cut along
the folded edge.

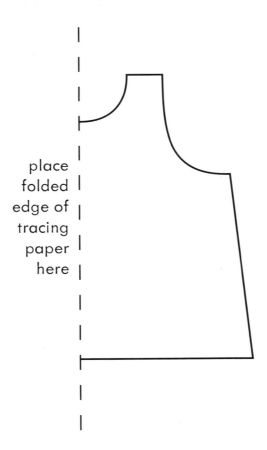

place
folded
edge of
tracing
paper
here

actual-size pattern

When you unfold the pattern,
the shape will look like this.

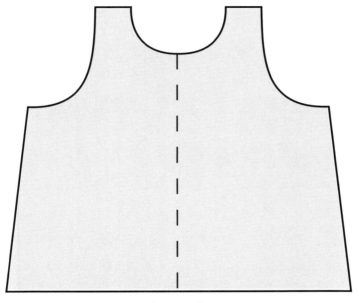

this is the
fold line

Now fold the fabric in half.

Place the top of your pattern
on the folded edge of the fabric.

Pin the pattern to the fabric.

Cut around the edge of the pattern.
Don't cut along the folded edge
of the fabric.

Then carefully cut out the neckhole.
Make sure you don't cut into the
fabric on either side of it.

this is the folded edge

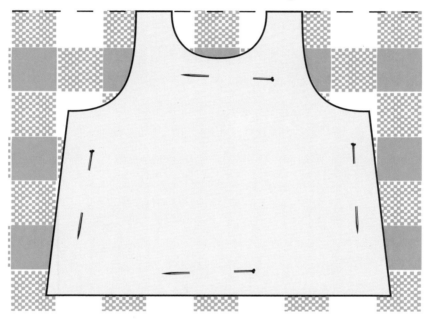

Take out the pins and lift
the pattern off the fabric.

This is the shape of the fabric
when it's opened out.

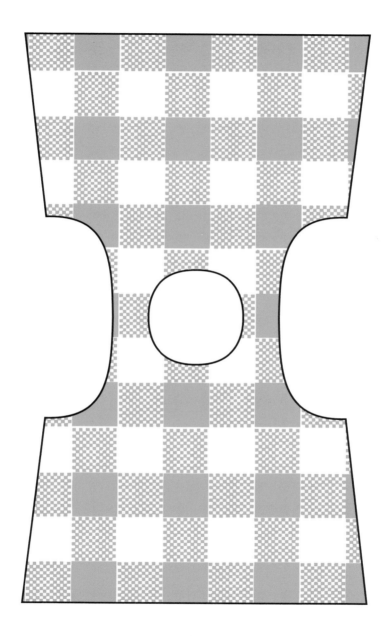

Fold your shape with the pretty sides together. Then pin the pieces together.

Now you are ready to sew.

Sew the fabric together along the two sides.

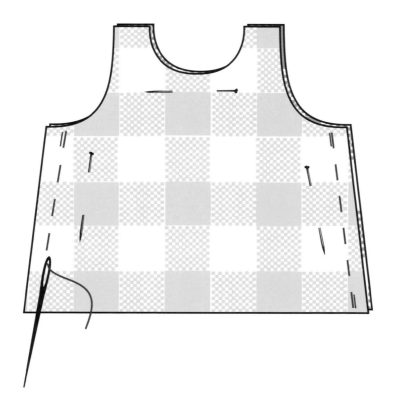

Turn it pretty side out.

To make a back opening,
cut up the middle. Make sure
to cut through just the top layer
of fabric.

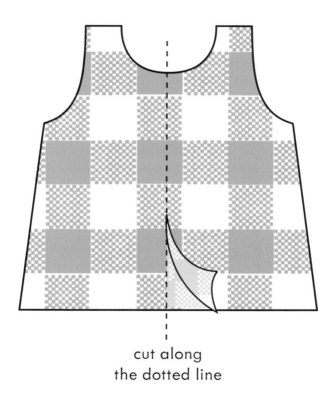

cut along
the dotted line

Sew the snap onto the top
of the opening.

back

Sew the ric-rac all around
the bottom edge.

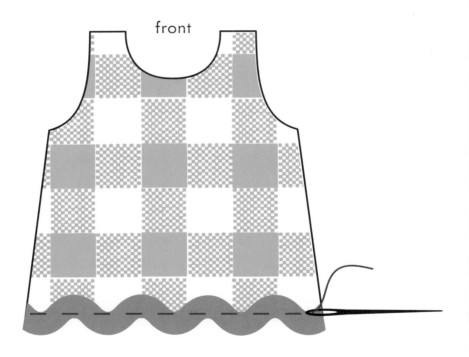

front

Sew the button onto the front.
Your doll's top is finished.

a knee-length coat

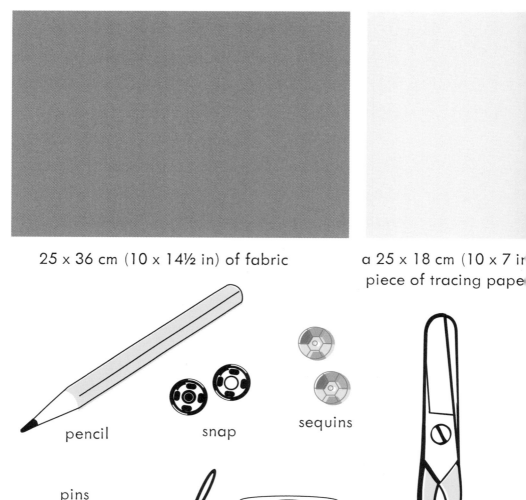

25 x 36 cm (10 x 14½ in) of fabric

a 25 x 18 cm (10 x 7 in) piece of tracing paper

pencil

snap

sequins

pins

needle

sewing thread

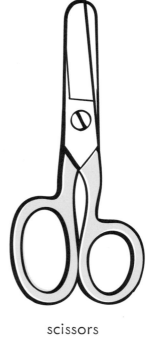

scissors

you will need

a piece of fabric

some tracing paper

a pencil

a snap

some sequins

some pins

a needle

sewing thread

and a pair of scissors

First you need to make a pattern.

Fold the tracing paper in half.

Place the folded edge against
the dotted line on the page.

Carefully trace the outline on
the page onto the tracing paper.

Cut around the solid line on the
tracing paper. Don't cut along
the folded edge.

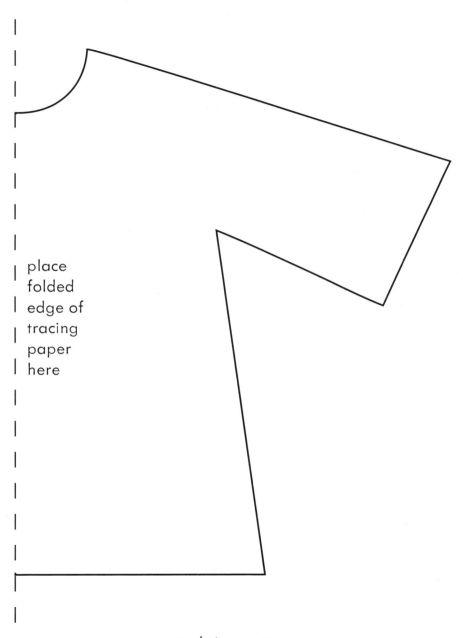

place
folded
edge of
tracing
paper
here

actual-size pattern

When you unfold the pattern,
the shape will look like this.

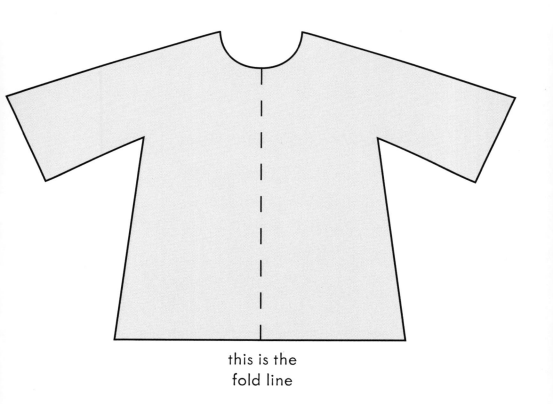

this is the
fold line

Now fold the fabric in half.

Pin the pattern to the fabric.

Cut all around the edge of the pattern. Make sure you cut through both layers of fabric.

Then take out the pins and lift off the pattern.

this is the folded edge

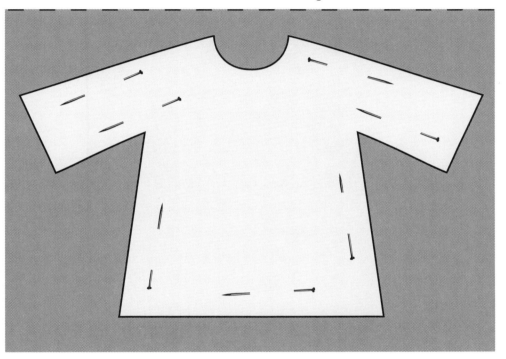

Pin the two pieces of fabric together. Make sure the pretty sides are facing each other.

Now you are ready to sew.

Sew the fabric together along the two sides and along the sleeves.

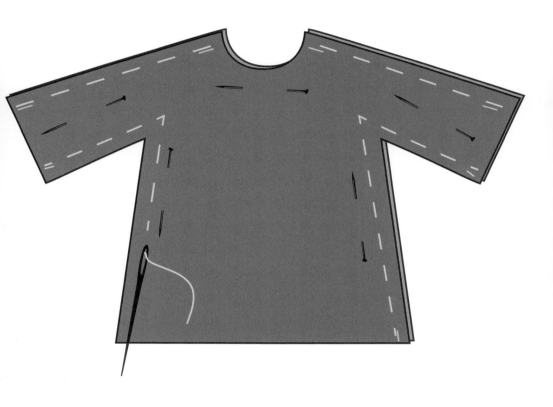

Turn it pretty side out.

To make a front opening,
cut up the middle. Make sure
to cut through just the top layer
of fabric.

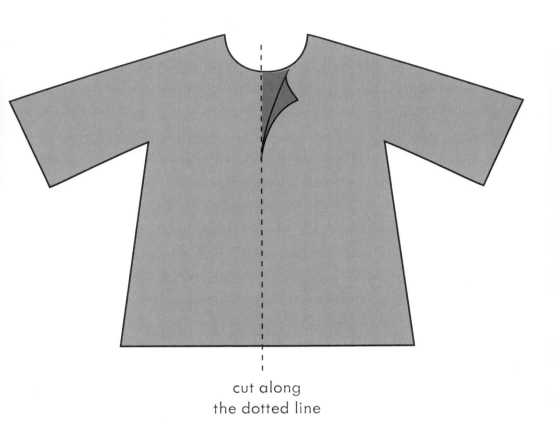

cut along
the dotted line

Sew the snap onto the top
of the front opening.

front

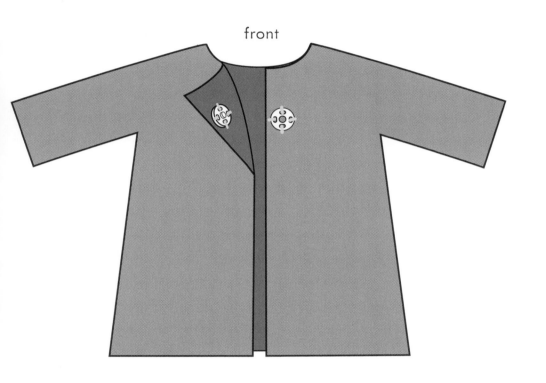

Now make the pockets.

Trace the pocket pattern on the page onto the leftover tracing paper. Cut it out.

Pin your pocket pattern onto the leftover fabric.

Cut out the pocket shape. You will need two pockets.

Sew the pockets onto the front of the coat.

actual-size pocket pattern

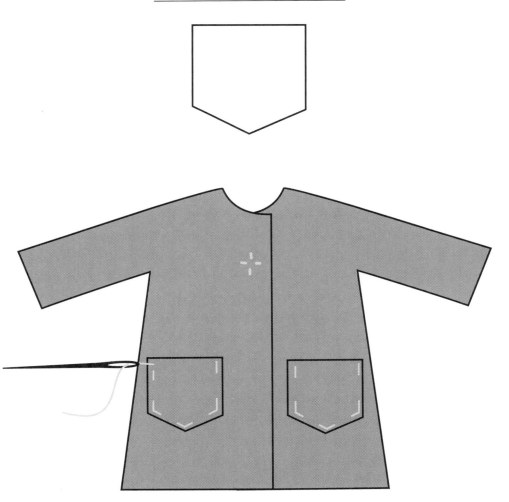

Sew on the sequins with a stitch
or two. Your doll's coat is finished.

an A-line skirt

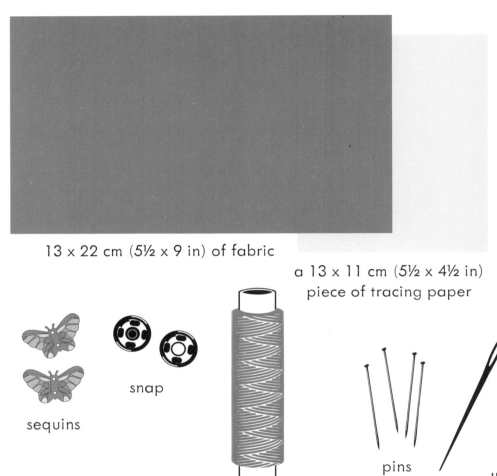

13 x 22 cm (5½ x 9 in) of fabric

a 13 x 11 cm (5½ x 4½ in)
piece of tracing paper

sequins

snap

sewing thread

pins

needle

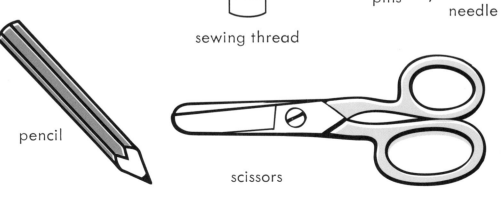

pencil

scissors

you will need

a piece of fabric

some tracing paper

some sequins

a snap

sewing thread

some pins

a needle

a pencil

and a pair of scissors

First you need to make a pattern.

Fold the tracing paper in half.

Place the folded edge against
the dotted line on the page.

Carefully trace the outline on
the page onto the tracing paper.

Cut around the solid line on the
tracing paper. Don't cut along
the folded edge.

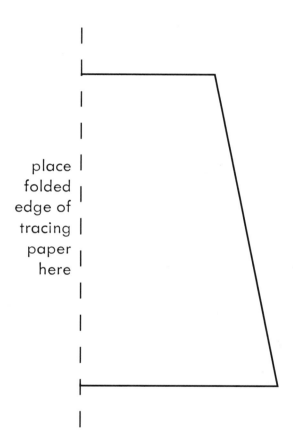

place
folded
edge of
tracing
paper
here

<u>actual-size pattern</u>

When you unfold the pattern,
the shape will look like this.

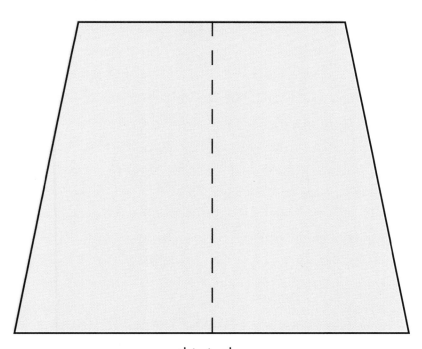

this is the
fold line

Now fold the fabric in half.

Pin the pattern to the fabric.

Cut all around the edge of the pattern. Make sure you cut through both layers of fabric.

Then take out the pins and lift off the pattern.

this is the folded edge

Pin the two pieces of fabric together. Make sure the pretty sides are facing each other.

Now you are ready to sew.

Sew the fabric together along the two sides.

Turn it pretty side out.

To make a back opening, cut down
the middle about 2.5 cm (1 in).
Make sure to cut through just
the top layer of fabric.

cut along
the dotted line

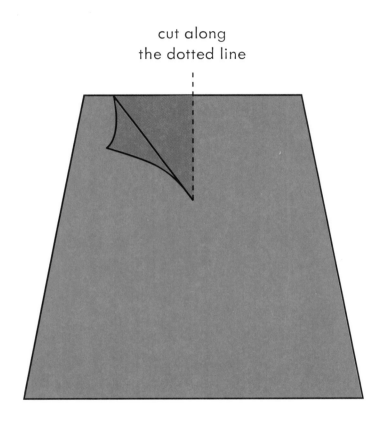

Sew the snap onto the top
of the back opening.

back

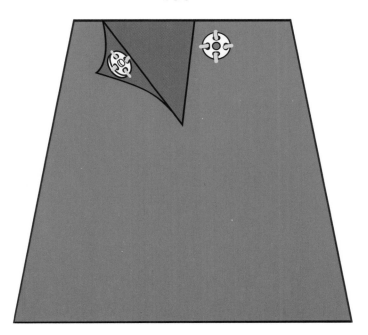

Sew on some sequins to decorate.
Your doll's A-line skirt is finished.

a faux-fur jacket

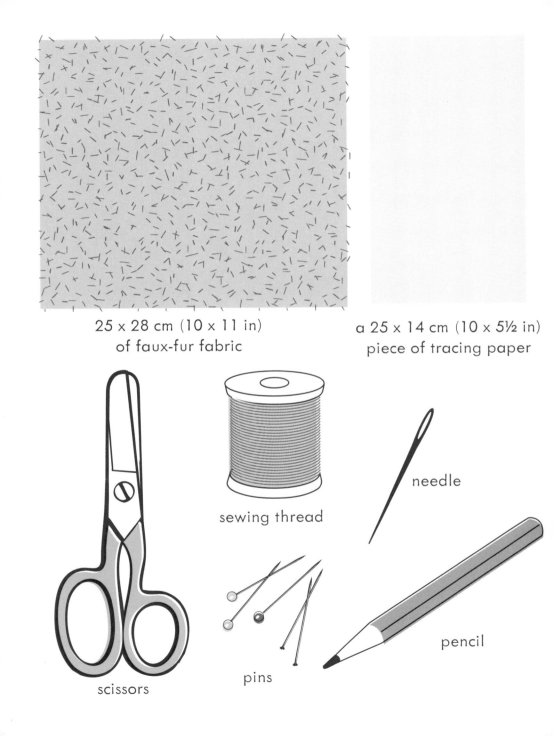

25 x 28 cm (10 x 11 in)
of faux-fur fabric

a 25 x 14 cm (10 x 5½ in)
piece of tracing paper

sewing thread

needle

pencil

scissors

pins

you will need

a piece of fabric

some tracing paper

a pair of scissors

sewing thread

a needle

some pins

and a pencil

First you need to make a pattern.

Fold the tracing paper in half.

Place the folded edge against
the dotted line on the page.

Carefully trace the outline on
the page onto the tracing paper.

Cut around the solid line on the
tracing paper. Don't cut along
the folded edge.

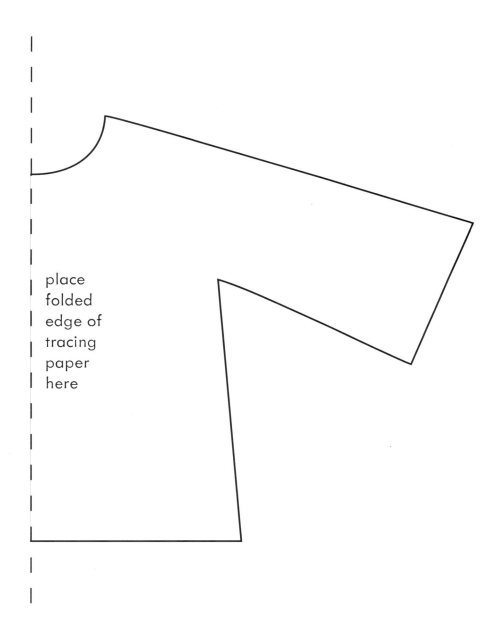

place
folded
edge of
tracing
paper
here

actual-size pattern

When you unfold the pattern,
the shape will look like this.

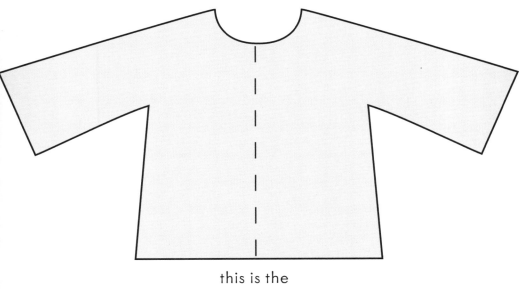

this is the
fold line

Now fold the fabric in half, fluffy sides together.

Pin the pattern to the fabric.

Cut all around the edge of the pattern. Make sure you cut through both layers of fabric.

Then take out the pins and lift off the pattern.

this is the folded edge

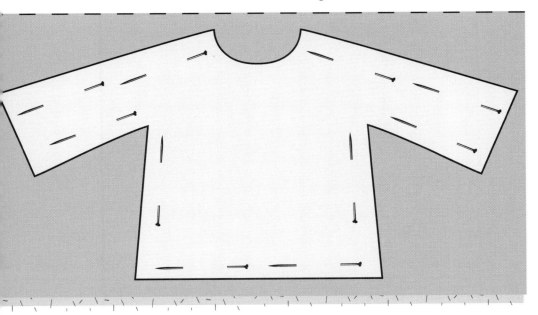

Pin the two pieces of fabric together. Make sure the fluffy sides are together.

Now you are ready to sew.

Sew the fabric together along the two sides and along the sleeves.

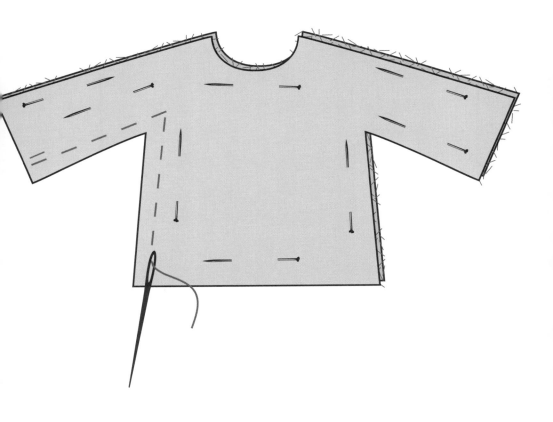

Turn it fluffy side out.

To make a front opening, cut up the middle. Make sure to cut through just the top layer of fabric.

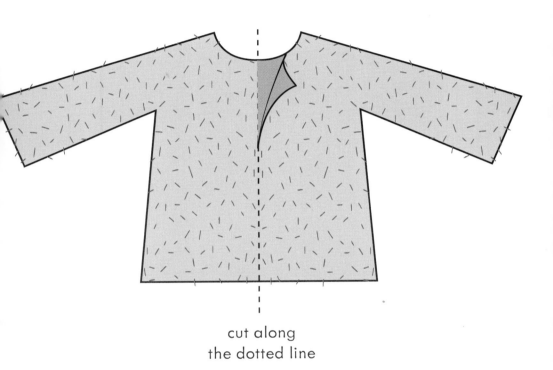

cut along
the dotted line

Your doll's faux-fur jacket is finished.

a skater skirt

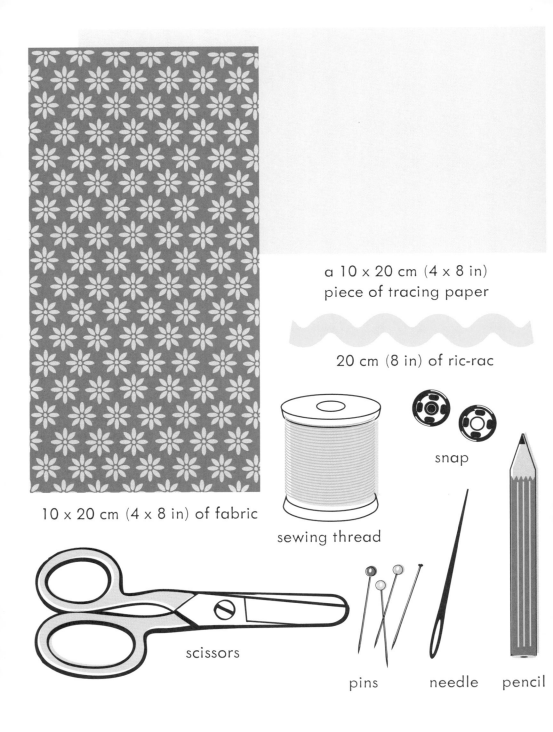

a 10 x 20 cm (4 x 8 in)
piece of tracing paper

20 cm (8 in) of ric-rac

snap

10 x 20 cm (4 x 8 in) of fabric

sewing thread

scissors

pins   needle   pencil

you will need

a piece of fabric

some tracing paper

some ric-rac

sewing thread

a snap

a pair of scissors

some pins

a needle

and a pencil

First you need to make a pattern.

Fold the tracing paper in half.

Place the folded edge against
the dotted line on the page.

Carefully trace the outline on
the page onto the tracing paper.

Cut around the solid line on the
tracing paper. Don't cut along
the folded edge.

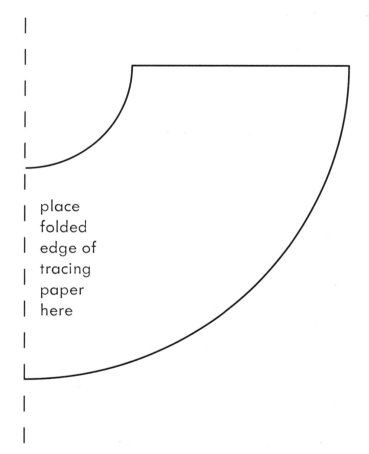

place
folded
edge of
tracing
paper
here

actual-size pattern

When you unfold the pattern,
the shape will look like this.

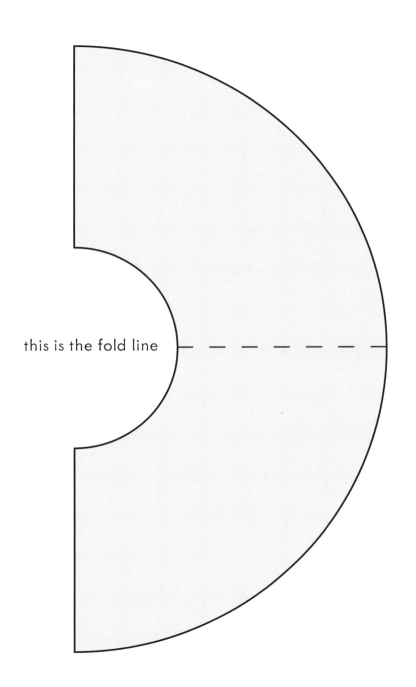

this is the fold line

Pin the pattern to the fabric.

Cut all around the edge of
the pattern.

Take out the pins and lift off
the pattern.

Fold the piece of fabric in half
and pin the two halves together.
Make sure the pretty sides are
facing each other.

Now you are ready to sew.

Sew the fabric together along the
straight edge. Leave an opening
of about 2.5 cm (1 in) at the top.

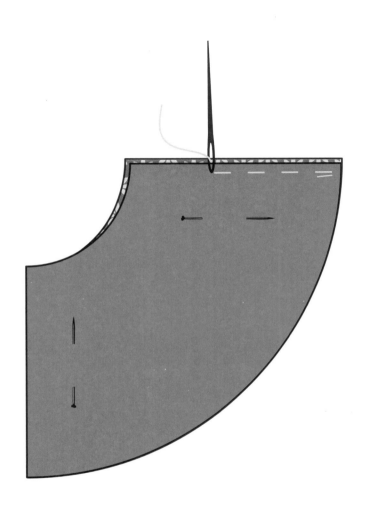

Turn it pretty side out.

Sew the snap onto the
top of the opening.

Sew on some ric-rac to decorate.

Your doll's skirt is finished.

a day dress

12 x 28 cm (5 x 11 in) of fabric

a 12 x 14 cm (5 x 5½ in)
piece of tracing paper

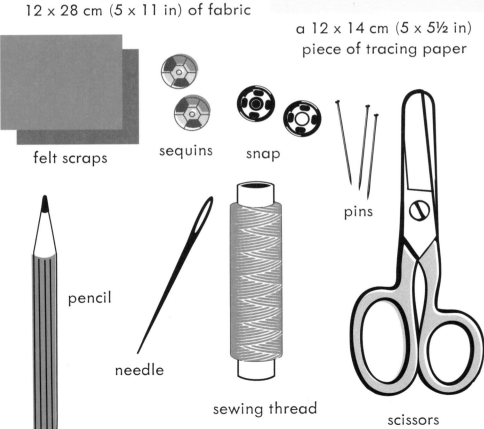

felt scraps

sequins

snap

pins

pencil

needle

sewing thread

scissors

you will need

a piece of fabric

some tracing paper

some felt scraps

some sequins

a snap

some pins

a pencil

a needle

sewing thread

and a pair of scissors

First you need to make a pattern.

Fold the tracing paper in half.

Place the folded edge against
the dotted line on the page.

Carefully trace the outline on
the page onto the tracing paper.

Cut around the solid line on the
tracing paper. Don't cut along
the folded edge.

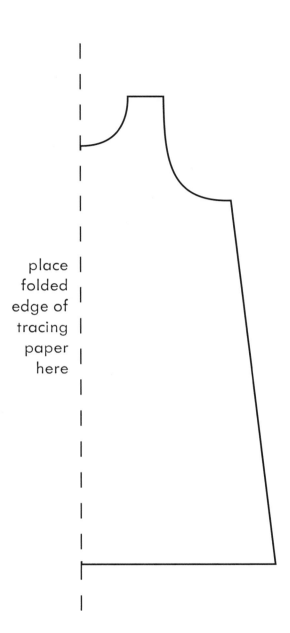

place
folded
edge of
tracing
paper
here

actual-size pattern

When you unfold the pattern,
the shape will look like this.

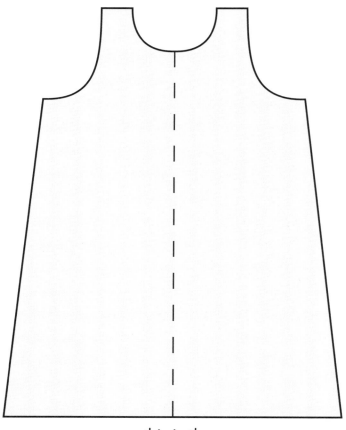

this is the
fold line

Now make patterns for the collar
and pocket of the dress.

Carefully trace the outlines on the
page onto the leftover tracing paper.

Cut out the shapes.

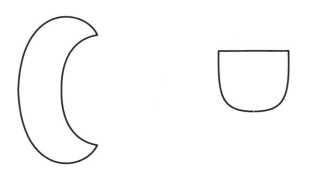

Now fold the fabric in half.

Place the top of your pattern
on the folded edge of the fabric.

Pin the pattern to the fabric.

Cut around the edge of the pattern.
Don't cut along the folded edge of
the fabric.

Then carefully cut out the neckhole.
Make sure you don't cut into the
fabric on either side of it.

this is the folded edge

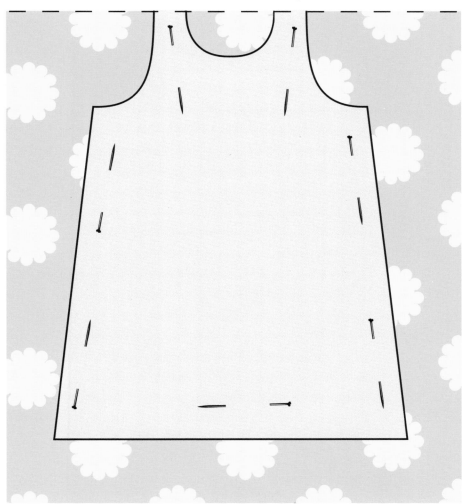

Take out the pins and lift
the pattern off the fabric.

This is the shape of the fabric
when it's opened out.

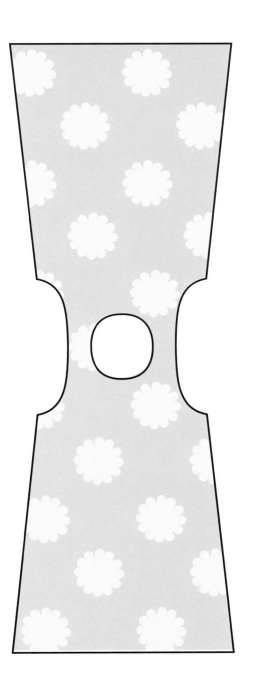

Fold your shape with the pretty sides facing each other. Then pin the pieces together.

Now you are ready to sew.

Sew the fabric together along the two sides.

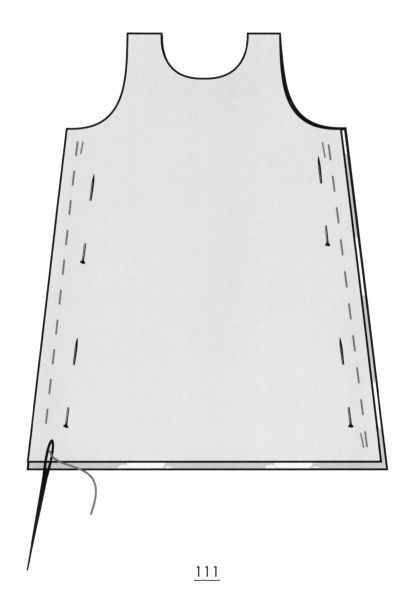

Turn it pretty side out.

To make a back opening, cut down
the middle about 5 cm (2 in).
Make sure to cut through just
the top layer of fabric.

cut along
the dotted
line

Sew the snap onto the top
of the opening.

Pin the collar and pocket patterns to your felt.

Cut all around the edges. You need two collar shapes and one pocket.

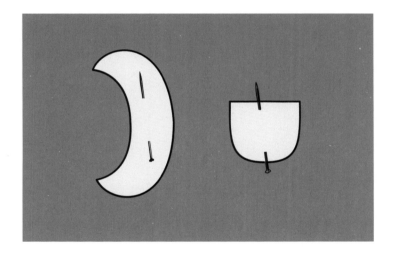

Sew the collar and pocket onto your dress.

Sew on some sequins to decorate.
Your doll's day dress is finished.

a party dress

flower moti[f]

a 3 x 7 cm (1½ x 3 in)
piece of tracing paper

a 3 x 14 cm (1½ x 5½ in)
piece of felt

Velcro patch

sewing thread

needle

scissors

pins

30 x 10 cm (12 x 4 in) of fabric

pencil

you will need

a piece of fabric

some tracing paper

a flower motif

a piece of felt

a Velcro patch

sewing thread

a pair of scissors

a pencil

a needle

and some pins

First you need to make a pattern
for the bodice of your dress.

Carefully trace the outline on
the page onto the tracing paper.

Cut around the line on the
tracing paper.

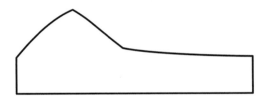

actual-size pattern

Fold the felt in half.

Pin the pattern to the felt. Make sure
the wider end of the pattern is next
to the folded edge of the felt.

Cut around the edge of the pattern.
Don't cut along the folded edge
of the felt.

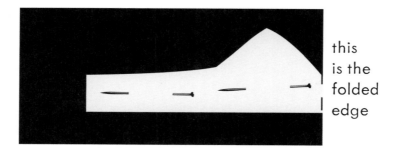

this
is the
folded
edge

Take out the pins and lift the pattern off the fabric.

This is the shape of the fabric when it's opened out.

Now you need to make the skirt
for your dress.

Sew a row of stitches along the top
edge of the fabric. Make sure to use
a running stitch (see page 169).

Leave long ends of thread at
each end of the seam.

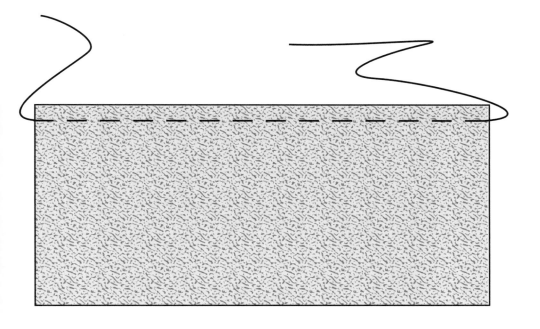

Gently pull both thread ends
to gather up the skirt. Do this
until the top of the skirt is just
a bit narrower than the bodice.

Then knot the threads securely
at each side and snip off the ends.

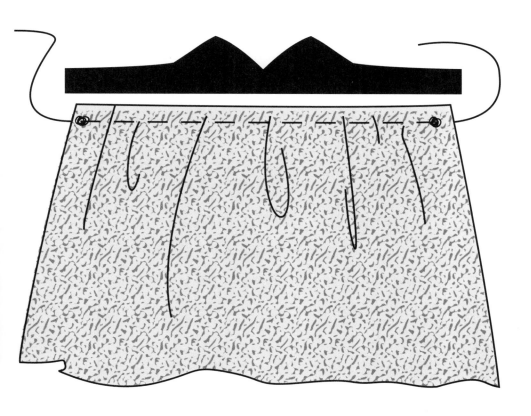

Pin the felt bodice along the
top edge of the gathered skirt.

Sew the felt and fabric together
along the bottom edge of the bodice.
Start and finish your stitching on
the wrong side of the fabric.

Make sure to leave a little bit of the
bodice sticking out on each side.

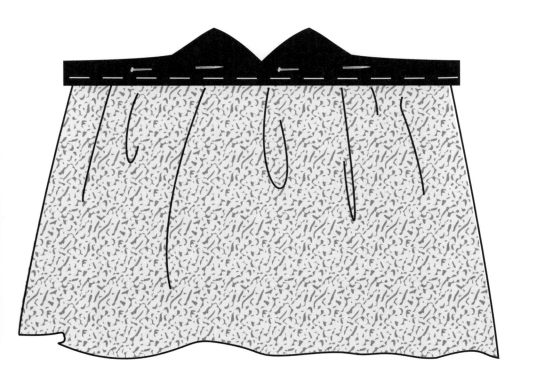

Fold the dress with the pretty sides facing each other. Then pin the pieces together.

Sew the skirt together up the straight edges of the fabric. Leave an opening of about 4 cm (1½ in) at the top.

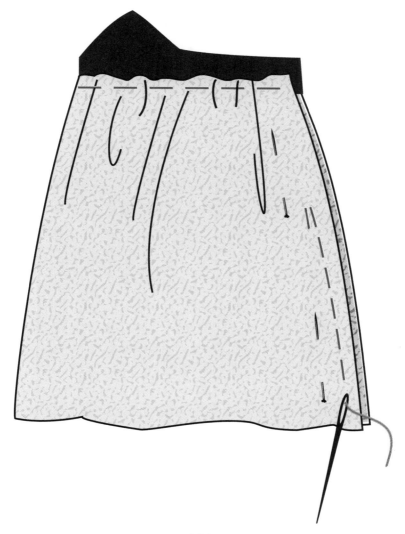

Turn the dress pretty side out.

Sew the Velcro patch onto
the top of the back opening.

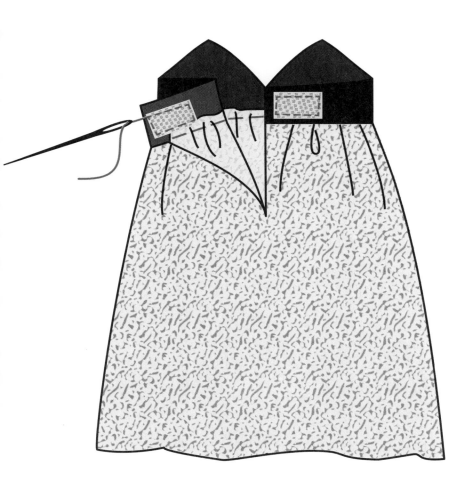

Sew the flower motif onto the front of the bodice.

Your doll's party dress is finished.

an evening bag

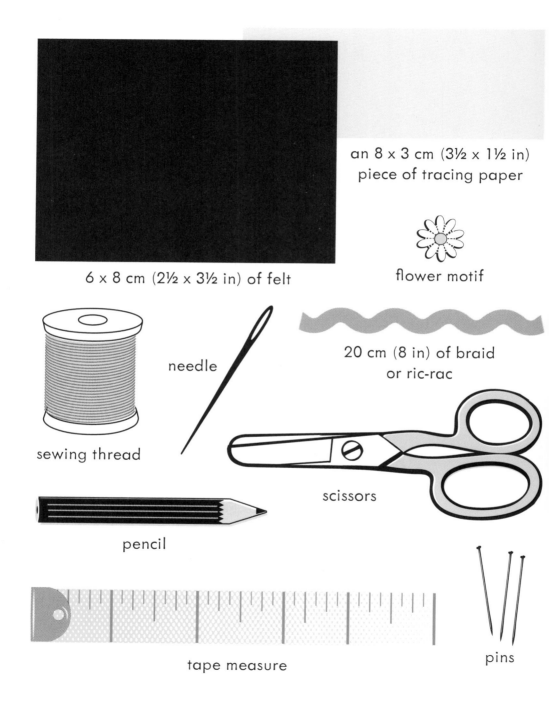

an 8 x 3 cm (3½ x 1½ in)
piece of tracing paper

flower motif

6 x 8 cm (2½ x 3½ in) of felt

20 cm (8 in) of braid
or ric-rac

needle

sewing thread

scissors

pencil

tape measure

pins

you will need

a piece of felt

some tracing paper

a flower motif

sewing thread

a needle

some braid or ric-rac

a pencil

a pair of scissors

a tape measure

and some pins

First you need to make a pattern.

Carefully trace the outline on
the page onto the tracing paper.

Cut around the line on the
tracing paper.

actual-size pattern

Now fold the felt in half.

Pin the pattern to the felt. Make sure the straight edge of the pattern is along the folded edge of the felt.

Cut around the edge of the pattern. Don't cut along the folded edge of the felt.

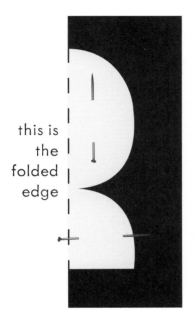

this is
the
folded
edge

Take out the pins and lift the pattern off the felt.

This is the shape of the felt when it's opened out.

Pin your shape together by folding
up the half-circle part of it.

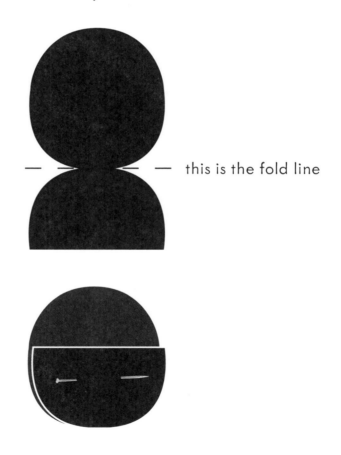

this is the fold line

Now you are ready to sew.

Sew the felt together along the
bottom edge of the half-circle.

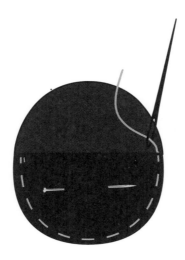

Now you need to add the bag strap.

Tuck the ends of your braid or ric-rac just inside the top corners of the bag.

Sew down the ends with two stitches. Knot the thread ends securely.

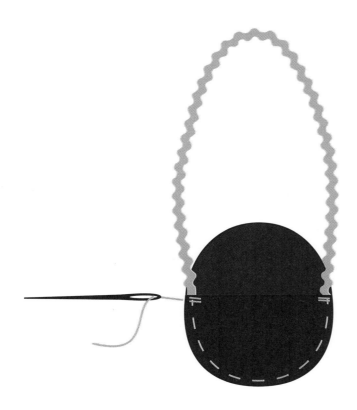

Sew a flower motif onto the front.

Your doll's evening bag is finished.

a fringed bag

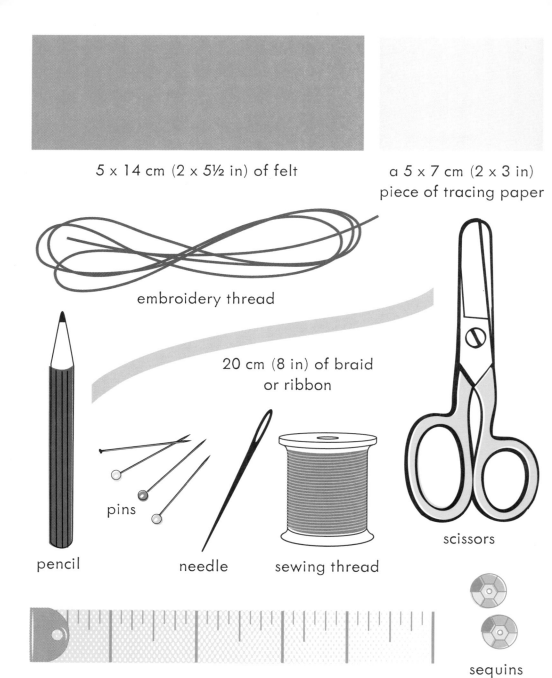

5 x 14 cm (2 x 5½ in) of felt

a 5 x 7 cm (2 x 3 in) piece of tracing paper

embroidery thread

20 cm (8 in) of braid or ribbon

pins

pencil

needle

sewing thread

scissors

sequins

tape measure

you will need

a piece of felt

some tracing paper

embroidery thread

a pencil

some braid or ribbon

a pair of scissors

some pins

a needle

sewing thread

a tape measure

and some sequins

First you need to make a pattern.

Carefully trace the outline and
the dotted lines of this picture
onto the tracing paper.

Cut around the solid outline.
Don't cut along the dotted lines.

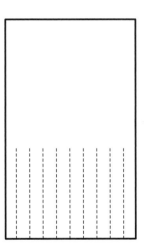

actual-size pattern

Now fold the felt in half.

Pin the pattern to the felt.

Cut around the edges of the pattern. Then cut up the dotted lines to make the fringe.

Take out the pins and lift off the pattern.

this is
the
folded
edge

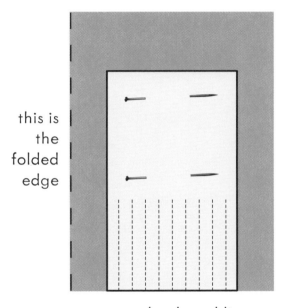

cut up the dotted lines

Use the embroidery thread to decorate one of your felt pieces with cross stitching. Sew on some sequins, too.

Pin the two pieces of felt together. Make sure the decorated side of the front piece is on the outside.

Sew the front and back pieces together. Don't sew along the top edge.

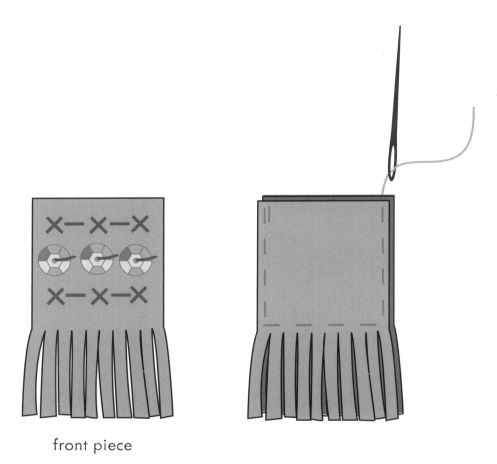

front piece

Sew down both ends of the braid strap just inside the top corners of the bag.

Your doll's fringed bag is finished.

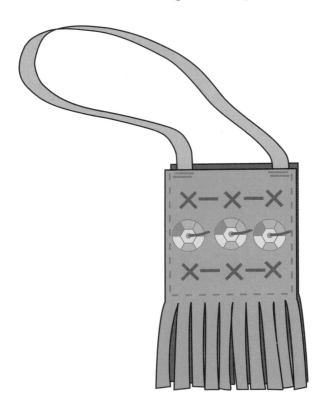

let's design

Now you can make your own dolls' clothes, why not have some fun creating your own designs?

Try adapting the patterns in this book. Make your skirt pattern longer, make your dress pattern shorter. Add a cute pocket, a collar, some embroidery or even some jewels!

Here are some ideas to get you started ...

Try using different buttons and braids. You can create a range of designs from the same basic pattern.

cut here

Make the A-line skirt pattern (page 49) shorter.
Add some cute pockets. Cut the bottom edge with
zig-zag scissors to give the skirt a pretty edge.

Or decorate the A-line skirt with some cute braid,
sequins and cross-stitch embroidery.

Experiment with prints. Different-sized prints can give the same dress a whole new look.

Sew on some glittery ric-rac and a vintage jewel to make a party version of the dress on page 99.

Unusual fabric choices can make your designs unique.

Use some pink-tinted clear plastic to make a rain coat from the knee-length coat pattern on page 29.

You're a designer now, so have fun with your creations and find your own style!

Use your sewing skills and imagination to create a truly one-of-a-kind wardrobe for your favorite doll.

first sewing steps

threading your needle

1. Cut off about 45 cm (18 in) of your sewing thread. Thread one end through the hole in your needle. Tie a knot at that end of the thread.

2. Tie another knot on top to make one big knot. Snip off the thread ends close to the knot. Leave the other end of the thread hanging loose on one side of the needle.

double-threading your needle

As your sewing gets better, try double-threading your needle. This makes your stitches stronger.

1. Cut off about 90 cm (35 in) of sewing thread. Thread one end through the hole in your needle.

2. Tie the ends of the thread together in one big knot.

running stitch

At first, sew your seams with a simple running stitch. Leave about 0.5 cm (¼ in) space between your seam and the edge of the fabric. This is your seam allowance.

1. Poke the needle up through the fabric. Gently pull until the knot stops the thread. Sew two stitches on top of each other at the start of your seam.

2. Make each stitch by pushing the needle down through both layers of fabric and then back up again a little further along. Make your stitches quite small and all the same size.

3. At the end of your seam, sew two stitches on top of each other. Knot your thread and snip off the ends.

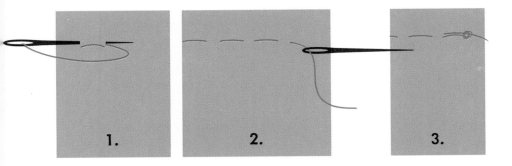

1.   **2.**   **3.**

back stitch

As your sewing gets better, try sewing your seams with back stitch. It is stronger than a running stitch.

1. Sew one stitch and bring your needle up ready to sew the second—just like running stitch.

2. Instead of sewing forward along the seam, as in a running stitch, go back and poke your needle down at the end of your first stitch.

3. Then bring your needle up two stitch lengths further along. Sew back down at the end of your previous stitch. Repeat until you reach the end.

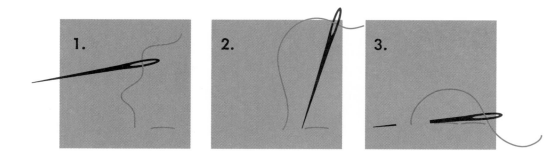

sewing on buttons

1. Knot the end of your thread. Hold the button against the fabric.

2. Bring your threaded needle up through the fabric and through one of the holes in the button. Pull the thread so the knot is tight against the fabric.

3. Sew back down through a different hole in the button. Repeat the stitch two or three times. To finish, knot the thread on the wrong side of the fabric.

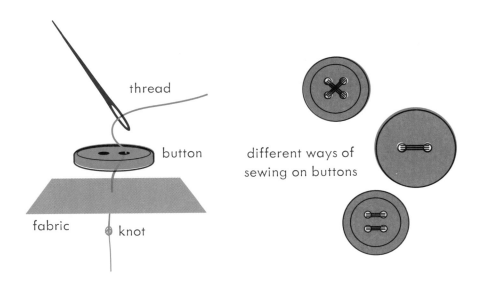

thread

button

fabric

knot

different ways of
sewing on buttons

sewing on snaps

A snap has two halves that fit together.
Make sure each one is in the right place and
is the right way up before you start sewing.

1. Make two stitches through the fabric where
you want to sew on your snap. Then poke your
threaded needle up through a hole in the snap.

2. Bring the needle back down through the fabric
at the outside edge of the snap.

3. Sew two or three stitches through each hole in
the snap. To finish, knot your thread at the back.

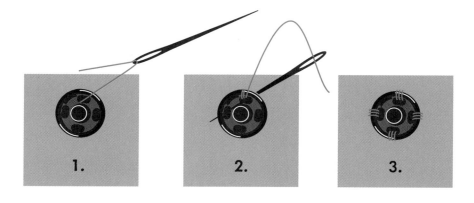

1. 2. 3.

cross stitch

You need to use thicker embroidery thread for cross stitch. Instead of doubling it up when you thread your needle, tie a big knot at one end and leave the other end loose through the needle.

1. Imagine the four corners of a square. Bring your needle up through the back of the fabric in one corner. Make a diagonal stitch to the opposite corner.

2. Continue in an even row along your fabric.

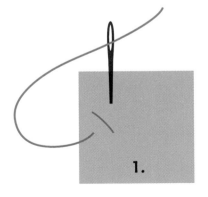
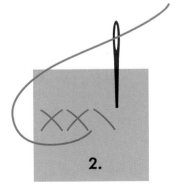

tips and tricks

ironing

Ask a grown-up to use an iron to flatten the seams on your finished dolls' clothes. This will make the clothes look very neat.

❗ Do not use the iron yourself, as it is hot and it could burn you badly.

fraying

Some fabrics fray when you cut them, so the edges become very messy. You can fix this by painting some clear nail polish along the edges after ironing.

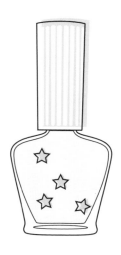

Felt is a great fabric to use because it doesn't fray. It is especially good for making collars, pockets and accessories.

clear nail polish

First published in the United Kingdom in 2015 by Thames & Hudson Ltd,
181A High Holborn, London WC1V 7QX

I Can Make Dolls' Clothes © 2015 Thames & Hudson Ltd, London

Created by Louise Scott-Smith and Georgia Vaux
Fashion design by Louise Scott-Smith
Graphic design by Georgia Vaux

All photographs by Pascal Bergamin

All the dolls used in this book are unbranded and the clothes are
the original works of the authors, except for some of the accessories.

First published in 2015 in hardcover in the United States of America by
Thames & Hudson Inc., 500 Fifth Avenue, New York, New York 10110

thamesandhudsonusa.com

Library of Congress Catalog Card Number 2015935383

ISBN 978-0-500-65051-6

Printed and bound in China by Everbest Printing Co. Ltd